The Westminster Confession of Faith: Journal Edition

Editors:
Shawn Anderson
Kyle Borg
Nathan Eshelman
Joel Wood

Copyright © 2017

Published by The Jerusalem Chamber Press
3557 Fletcher Drive
Los Angeles, CA 90065

credo ut intelligam

www.JerusalemChamber.com

TABLE OF CONTENTS

1. Of the Holy Scriptures — 4
2. Of God, and of the Holy Trinity — 24
3. Of God's Eternal Decree — 30
4. Of Creation — 46
5. Of Providence — 50
6. Of the Fall of Man, of Sin, and of the Punishment Thereof — 64
7. Of God's Covenant with Man — 76
8. Of Christ the Mediator — 88
9. Of Free Will — 104
10. Of Effectual Calling — 114
11. Of Justification — 122
12. Of Adoption — 134
13. Of Sanctification — 136
14. Of Saving Faith — 142
15. Of Repentance Unto Life — 148
16. Of Good Works — 160
17. Of the Perseverance of the Saints — 174
18. Of the Assurance of Grace and Salvation — 180
19. Of the Law of God — 188
20. Of Christian Liberty, and Liberty of Conscience — 202
21. Of Religious Worship, and the Sabbath Day — 210
22. Of Lawful Oaths and Vows — 226
23. Of the Civil Magistrate — 240
24. Of Marriage and Divorce — 248
25. Of the Church — 260
26. Of the Communion of the Saints — 272
27. Of the Sacraments — 278
28. Of Baptism — 288
29. Of the Lord's Supper — 302
30. Of Church Censures — 318
31. Of Synods and Councils — 326
32. Of the State of Men After Death, and the Resurrection of the Dead — 336
33. Of the Last Judgment — 342

CHAPTER 1:
OF THE HOLY SCRIPTURE

1.1. Although the light of nature, and the works of creation and providence, do so far manifest the goodness, wisdom, and power of God, as to leave men inexcusable; yet are they not sufficient to give that knowledge of God, and of his will, which is necessary unto salvation; therefore it pleased the Lord, at sundry times, and in divers manners, to reveal himself, and to declare that his will unto his Church; and afterwards for the better preserving and propagating of the truth, and for the more sure establishment and comfort of the Church against the corruption of the flesh, and the malice of Satan and of the world, to commit the same wholly unto writing; which maketh the holy Scripture to be most necessary; those former ways of God's revealing his will unto his people being now ceased.
Rom. 2:14-15; Rom. 1:19-20; Ps. 19:1-3; Rom. 1:32 with 2:1; 1 Cor. 1:21; 1 Cor. 2:13-14; Heb. 1:1; Prov. 22:19-21; Luke 1:3-4; Rom. 15:4; Matt. 4:4, 7, 10; Isa. 8:19-20; 2 Tim. 3:15; 2 Pet. 1:19; Heb. 1:1-2.

1.2. Under the name of Holy Scripture, or the Word of God written, are now contained all the books of the Old and New Testaments, which are these:

Of the Old Testament: Genesis; Exodus; Leviticus; Numbers; Deuteronomy; Joshua; Judges; Ruth; 1 Samuel; 2 Samuel; 1 Kings; 2 Kings; 1 Chronicles; 2 Chronicles; Ezra; Nehemiah; Esther; Job; Psalms; Proverbs; Ecclesiastes; The Song of Songs; Isaiah; Jeremiah; Lamentations; Ezekiel; Daniel; Hosea; Joel; Amos; Obadiah; Jonah; Micah; Nahum; Habakkuk; Zephaniah; Haggai; Zechariah; Malachi.

Of the New Testament: Matthew; Mark; Luke; John; Acts; Romans; 1 Corinthians; 2 Corinthians; Galatians; Ephesians; Philippians; Colossians; 1 Thessalonians; 2 Thessalonians; 1 Timothy; 2 Timothy; Titus; Philemon; Hebrews; James; 1 Peter; 2 Peter; 1 John; 2 John; 3 John; Jude; Revelation.

All which are given by inspiration of God, to be the rule of faith and life.

Luke 16:29, 31; Eph. 2:20; Rev. 22:18-19; 2 Tim. 3:16.

1.3. The books commonly called Apocrypha, not being of divine inspiration, are no part of the Canon of Scripture; and therefore are of no authority in the Church of God, nor to be any otherwise approved, or made use of, than other human writings.
Luke 24:27, 44; Rom. 3:2; 2 Pet. 1:21.

1.4. The authority of the Holy Scripture, for which it ought to be believed and obeyed, dependeth not upon the testimony of any man, or church; but wholly upon God (who is truth itself) the author thereof: and therefore it is to be received because it is the Word of God.
2 Pet. 1:19, 21; 2 Tim. 3:16; 1 John 5:9; 1 Thess. 2:13.

1.5. We may be moved and induced by the testimony of the Church to a high and reverent esteem of the Holy Scripture. And the heavenliness of the matter, the efficacy of the doctrine, the majesty of the style, the consent of all the parts, the scope of the whole (which is, to give all glory to God), the full discovery it makes of the only way of man's salvation, the many other incomparable excellencies, and the entire perfection thereof, are arguments whereby it doth abundantly evidence itself to be the Word of God: yet notwithstanding, our full persuasion and assurance of the infallible truth and divine authority thereof, is from the inward work of the Holy Spirit bearing witness by and with the Word in our hearts.
1 Tim. 3:15; 1 John 2:20, 27; John 16:13-14; 1 Cor. 2:10-12; Isa. 59:21.

1.6. The whole counsel of God concerning all things necessary for His own glory, man's salvation, faith, and life, is either expressly set down in Scripture, or by good and necessary consequence may be deduced from Scripture: unto which nothing at any time is to be added, whether by new revelations of the Spirit, or traditions of men. Nevertheless we acknowledge the inward illumination of the Spirit of God to be necessary for the saving understanding of such things as are revealed in the Word: and that there are some circumstances concerning the worship of God, and government of the Church, common to human actions and societies, which are to be ordered by the light of nature and Christian prudence, according to the general rules of the Word, which are always to be observed.
2 Tim. 3:15-17; Gal. 1:8-9; 2 Thess. 2:2; John 6:45; 1 Cor. 2:9-12; 1 Cor. 11:13-14; 1 Cor. 14:26, 40.

1.7. All things in Scripture are not alike plain in themselves, nor alike clear unto all: yet those things which are necessary to be known, believed, and observed for salvation, are so clearly propounded and opened in some place of Scripture or other, that not only the learned, but the unlearned, in a due use of the ordinary means, may attain unto a sufficient understanding of them. *2 Pet. 3:16; Ps. 119:105, 130.*

1.8. The Old Testament in Hebrew (which was the native language of the people of God of old), and the New Testament in Greek (which at the time of the writing of it was most generally known to the nations), being immediately inspired by God, and by His singular care and providence kept pure in all ages, are therefore authentical; so as, in all controversies of religion, the Church is finally to appeal unto them. But, because these original tongues are not known to all the people of God, who have a right unto, and interest in the Scriptures, and are commanded, in the fear of God, to read and search them, therefore they are to be translated into the vulgar language of every nation unto which they come, that the Word of God dwelling plentifully in all, they may worship Him in an acceptable manner; and, through patience and comfort of the Scriptures, may have hope.
Matt. 5:18; Isa. 8:20; Acts 15:15; John 5:39, 46; 1 Cor. 14:6, 9, 11-12, 24, 27-28; Col. 3:16; Rom. 15:4.

1.9. The infallible rule of interpretation of Scripture is the Scripture itself: and therefore, when there is a question about the true and full sense of any Scripture (which is not manifold, but one) it must be searched and known by other places that speak more clearly.
2 Pet. 1:20-21; Acts 15:15-16.

1.10. The supreme judge by which all controversies of religion are to be determined, and all decrees of councils, opinions of ancient writers, doctrines of men, and private spirits, are to be examined; and in whose sentence we are to rest; can be no other but the Holy Spirit speaking in the Scripture.
Matt. 22:29, 31; Eph. 2:20 with Acts 28:25.

CHAPTER 2:
OF GOD, AND OF THE HOLY TRINITY

2.1. There is but one only, living, and true God: who is infinite in being and perfection, a most pure spirit, invisible, without body, parts, or passions, immutable, immense, eternal, incomprehensible, almighty, most wise, most holy, most free, most absolute, working all things according to the counsel of His own immutable and most righteous will, for His own glory; most loving, gracious, merciful, long-suffering, abundant in goodness and truth, forgiving iniquity, transgression, and sin; the rewarder of them that diligently seek Him; and withal, most just and terrible in His judgments, hating all sin, and who will by no means clear the guilty.
Deut. 6:4, 1 Cor. 8:4, 6; 1 Thess. 1:9; Jer. 10:10; Job 11:7-9; Job 26:14; John 4:24; 1 Tim. 1:17; Deut. 4:15-16; John 4:24 with Luke 24:39; Acts 14:11, 15; Jas. 1:17; Mal. 3:6; 1 Kings 8:27; Jer. 23: 23-24; Ps. 90:2; 1 Tim. 1:17; Ps. 145:3; Gen. 17:1; Rev. 4:8; Rom. 16:27; Isa. 6:3; Rev. 4:8; Ps. 115:3; Ex. 3:14; Eph. 1:11; Prov. 16:4; Rom. 11:36; 1 John 4:8, 16; Ex. 34:6-7; Heb. 11:6; Neh. 9:32-33; Ps. 5:5-6; Nah. 1:2-3; Ex. 34:7.

2.2. God hath all life, glory, goodness, blessedness, in and of Himself; and is alone in and unto Himself all-sufficient, not standing in need of any creatures which He hath made, nor deriving any glory from them, but only manifesting His own glory in, by, unto, and upon them: He is the alone fountain of all being, of whom, through whom, and to whom are all things; and hath most sovereign dominion over them, to do by them, for them, or upon them whatsoever Himself pleaseth. In His sight all things are open and manifest; His knowledge is infinite, infallible, and independent upon the creature, so as nothing is to Him contingent, or uncertain. He is most holy in all His counsels, in all His works, and in all His commands. To Him is due from angels and men, and every other creature, whatsoever worship, service or obedience He is pleased to require of them.
John 5:26; Acts 7:2; Ps. 119:68; 1 Tim. 6:15; Rom. 9:5; Acts 17:24-25; Job 22:2-3; Rom. 11:36; Rev. 4:11; 1 Tim. 6:15; Dan. 4:25, 35; Heb. 4:13; Rom. 11:33-34; Ps. 147:5; Acts 15:18; Ezek. 11:5; Ps. 145:17; Rom. 7:12; Rev. 5:12-14.

2.3. In the unity of the Godhead there be three persons, of one substance, power, and eternity; God the Father, God the Son, and God the Holy Ghost. The Father is of none, neither begotten, nor proceeding: the Son is eternally begotten of the Father: the Holy Ghost eternally proceeding from the Father and the Son.
1 John 5:7; Matt. 3:16-17; Matt. 28:19; 2 Cor. 13:14; John 1:14, 18; John 15:26; Gal. 4:6.

CHAPTER 3:
OF GOD'S ETERNAL DECREE

3.1. God from all eternity did, by the most wise and holy counsel of His own will, freely, and unchangeably ordain whatsoever comes to pass: yet so, as thereby neither is God the author of sin, nor is violence offered to the will of the creatures, nor is the liberty or contingency of second causes taken away, but rather established.

Eph. 1:11; Rom. 11:33; Heb. 6:17; Rom. 9:15, 18; Jas. 1:13, 17; 1 John 1:5; Acts 2:23; Matt. 17:12; Acts 4:27-28; John 19:11; Prov. 16:33.

3.2. Although God knows whatsoever may or can come to pass upon all supposed conditions, yet hath He not decreed anything because He foresaw it as future, or as that which would come to pass upon such conditions.
Acts 15:18; 1 Sam. 23:11-12; Matt. 11:21, 23; Rom. 9:11, 13, 16, 18.

3.3. By the decree of God, for the manifestation of His glory, some men and angels are predestinated unto everlasting life, and others fore-ordained to everlasting death.
1 Tim. 5:21; Matt. 25:41; Rom. 9:22-23; Eph. 1:5-6; Prov. 16:4.

3.4. These angels and men, thus predestinated and fore-ordained, are particularly and unchangeably designed, and their number is so certain and definite, that it cannot be either increased or diminished.
2 Tim. 2:19; John 13:18.

3.5. Those of mankind that are predestinated unto life, God, before the foundation of the world was laid, according to His eternal and immutable purpose, and the secret counsel and good pleasure of His will, hath chosen, in Christ, unto everlasting glory, out of His mere free grace and love, without any foresight of faith or good works, or perseverance in either of them, or any other thing in the creature, as conditions, or causes moving Him thereunto: and all to the praise of His glorious grace.
Eph. 1:4, 9, 11; Rom. 8:30; 2 Tim. 1:9; 1 Thess. 5:9; Rom. 9:11, 13, 16; Eph. 1:4, 9; Eph. 1:6, 12.

3.6. As God hath appointed the elect unto glory, so hath He, by the eternal and most free purpose of His will, foreordained all the means thereunto. Wherefore they who are elected, being fallen in Adam, are redeemed by Christ, are effectually called unto faith in Christ by His Spirit working in due season, are justified, adopted, sanctified, and kept by His power through faith unto salvation. Neither are any other redeemed by Christ, effectually called, justified, adopted, sanctified, and saved, but the elect only.

1 Pet. 1:2; Eph. 1:4-5; Eph. 2:10; 2 Thess. 2:13; 1 Thess. 5:9-10; Titus 2:14; Rom. 8:30; Eph. 1:5; 2 Thess. 2:13; 1 Pet. 1:5; John 17:9; Rom. 8:28-39; John 6:64-65; John 10:26; John 8:47; 1 John 2:19.

3.7. The rest of mankind God was pleased, according to the unsearchable counsel of His own will, whereby He extendeth or withholdeth mercy, as He pleaseth, for the glory of His sovereign power over His creatures, to pass by; and to ordain them to dishonour and wrath, for their sin, to the praise of His glorious justice. *Matt. 11:25-26; Rom. 9:17-18, 21-22; 2 Tim. 2:19-20; Jude 1:4; 1 Pet. 2:8.*

3.8. The doctrine of this high mystery of predestination is to be handled with special prudence and care, that men attending the will of God revealed in His Word, and yielding obedience thereunto, may, from the certainty of their effectual vocation, be assured of their eternal election. So shall this doctrine afford matter of praise, reverence, and admiration of God, and of humility, diligence, and abundant consolation to all that sincerely obey the Gospel.
Rom. 9:20; Rom. 11:33; Deut. 29:29; 2 Pet. 1:10; Eph. 1:6; Rom. 11:33; Rom. 11:5-6, 20; 2 Pet. 1:10; Rom. 8:33; Luke 10:20.

CHAPTER 4:
OF CREATION

4.1. It pleased God the Father, Son, and Holy Ghost, for the manifestation of the glory of His eternal power, wisdom, and goodness, in the beginning, to create, or make of nothing, the world, and all things therein whether visible or invisible, in the space of six days; and all very good.
Heb. 1:2; John 1:2-3; Gen. 1:2; Job 26:13; Job 33:4; Rom. 1:20; Jer. 10:12; Ps. 104:24; Ps. 33:5-6; Gen. 1; Heb. 11:3; Col. 1:16; Acts 17:24.

4.2. After God had made all other creatures, He created man, male and female, with reasonable and immortal souls, endued with knowledge, righteousness, and true holiness, after His own image; having the law of God written in their hearts, and power to fulfil it: and yet under a possibility of transgressing, being left to the liberty of their own will, which was subject unto change. Beside this law written in their hearts, they received a command not to eat of the tree of the knowledge of good and evil, which while they kept, they were happy in their communion with God, and had dominion over the creatures.
Gen. 1:27; Gen. 2:7 with Eccl. 12:7, and Luke 23:43, and Matt. 10:28; Gen. 1:26; Col. 3:10; Eph. 4:24; Rom. 2:14-15; Eccl. 7:29; Gen. 3:6; Eccl. 7:29; Gen. 2:17; Gen. 3:8-11, 23; Gen. 1:26, 28.

CHAPTER 5:
OF PROVIDENCE

5.1. God the great Creator of all things doth uphold, direct, dispose, and govern all creatures, actions, and things, from the greatest even to the least, by His most wise and holy providence, according to His infallible fore-knowledge, and the free and immutable counsel of His own will, to the praise of the glory of His wisdom, power, justice, goodness and mercy.
Heb. 1:3; Dan. 4:34-35; Ps. 135:6; Acts 17:25-26, 28; Job 38—41; Matt. 10:29-31; Prov. 15:3; Ps. 104:24; Ps. 145:17; Acts 15:18; Ps. 94:8-11; Eph. 1:11; Ps. 33:10-11; Isa. 63:14; Eph. 3:10; Rom. 9:17; Gen. 45:7; Ps. 145:7.

5.2. Although, in relation to the foreknowledge and decree of God, the first Cause, all things come to pass immutably, and infallibly: yet, by the same providence, He ordereth them to fall out, according to the nature of second causes, either necessarily, freely, or contingently.

Acts 2:23; Gen. 8:22; Jer. 31:35; Ex. 21:13 with Deut. 19:5; 1 Kings 22:28, 34; Isa. 10:6-7.

5.3. God in His ordinary providence maketh use of means, yet is free to work without, above, and against them at His pleasure.
Acts 27:31, 44; Isa. 55:10-11; Hos. 2:21-22; Hos. 1:7; Matt. 4:4; Job 34:20; Rom. 4:19-21; 2 Kings 6:6; Dan. 3:27.

5.4. The almighty power, unsearchable wisdom, and infinite goodness of God so far manifest themselves in His providence, that it extendeth itself even to the first fall, and all other sins of angels and men; and that not by a bare permission, but such as hath joined with it a most wise and powerful bounding, and otherwise ordering and governing of them, in a manifold dispensation, to His own holy ends; yet so, as the sinfulness thereof proceedeth only from the creature, and not from God, who, being most holy and righteous, neither is, nor can be, the author or approver of sin.

Rom. 11:32-34; 2 Sam. 24:1 with 1 Chron. 21:1; 1 Kings 22:22-23; 1 Chron. 10:4, 13-14; 2 Sam. 16:10; Acts 2:23; Acts 4:27-28; Acts 14:16; Ps. 76:10; 2 Kings 19:28; Gen. 50:20; Isa. 10:6-7, 12; Jas. 1:13-14, 17; 1 John 2:16; Ps. 50:21.

Westminster Confession of Faith

5.5. The most wise, righteous, and gracious God doth oftentimes leave for a season His own children to manifold temptations, and the corruption of their own hearts, to chastise them for their former sins, or to discover unto them the hidden strength of corruption, and deceitfulness of their hearts, that they may be humbled; and, to raise them to a more close and constant dependence for their support upon Himself, and to make them more watchful against all future occasions of sin, and for sundry other just and holy ends.

2 Chron. 32:25-26, 31; 2 Sam. 24:1; 2 Cor. 12:7-9; Ps. 73; Ps. 77:1-12; Mark 14:66-72 with John 21:15-17.

5.6. As for those wicked and ungodly men whom God, as a righteous Judge, for former sins doth blind and harden, from them He not only withholdeth His grace, whereby they might have been enlightened in their understandings, and wrought upon in their hearts; but sometimes also withdraweth the gifts which they had, and exposeth them to such objects as their corruption makes occasions of sin; and, withal, gives them over to their own lusts, the temptations of the world, and the power of Satan: whereby it comes to pass that they harden themselves, even under those means which God useth for the softening of others.
Rom. 1:24, 26, 28; Rom. 11:7-8; Deut. 29:4; Matt. 13:12; Matt. 25:29; Deut. 2:30; 2 Kings 8:12-13; Ps. 81:11-12; 2 Thess. 2:10-12; Ex. 7:3 with Ex. 8:15, 32; 2 Cor. 2:15-16; Isa. 8:14; 1 Pet. 2:7-8; Isa. 6:9-10 with Acts 28:26-27.

5.7. As the providence of God doth in general reach to all creatures, so after a most special manner it taketh care of His Church, and disposeth all things to the good thereof.
1 Tim. 4:10; Amos 9:8-9; Rom. 8:28; Isa. 43:3-5, 14.

CHAPTER 6:
OF THE FALL OF MAN, OF SIN, AND OF THE PUNISHMENT THEREOF

6.1. Our first parents, being seduced by the subtilty and temptation of Satan, sinned in eating the forbidden fruit. This their sin God was pleased, according to His wise and holy counsel, to permit, having purposed to order it to His own glory.
Gen. 3:13; 2 Cor. 11:3; Rom. 11:32.

6.2. By this sin they fell from their original righteousness and communion with God, and so became dead in sin, and wholly defiled in all the faculties and parts of soul and body.
Gen. 3:6-8; Eccl. 7:29; Rom. 3:23; Gen. 2:17; Eph. 2:1; Titus 1:15; Gen. 6:5; Jer. 17:9; Rom. 3:10-19.

6.3. They being the root of all mankind, the guilt of this sin was imputed, and the same death in sin and corrupted nature conveyed, to all their posterity descending from them by ordinary generation.
Gen. 1:27-28, and Gen. 2:16-17, and Acts 17:26 with Rom. 5:12, 15-19, and 1 Cor. 15:21-22, 49; Ps. 51:5; Gen. 5:3; Job 14:4; Job 15:14.

6.4. From this original corruption, whereby we are utterly indisposed, disabled, and made opposite to all good, and wholly inclined to all evil, do proceed all actual transgressions.
Rom. 5:6; Rom. 8:7; Rom. 7:18; Col. 1:21; Gen. 6:5; Gen. 8:21; Rom. 3:10-12; Jas. 1:14-15; Eph. 2:2-3; Matt. 15:19.

6.5. This corruption of nature, during this life, doth remain in those that are regenerated; and although it be, through Christ, pardoned and mortified, yet both itself and all the motions thereof are truly and properly sin.
1 John 1:8, 10; Rom. 7:14, 17-18, 23; Jas. 3:2; Prov. 20:9; Eccl. 7:20; Rom. 7:5, 7-8, 25; Gal. 5:17.

6.6. Every sin, both original and actual, being a transgression of the righteous law of God, and contrary thereunto, doth, in its own nature, bring guilt upon the sinner; whereby he is bound over to the wrath of God, and curse of the law, and so made subject to death, with all miseries spiritual, temporal, and eternal.
1 John 3:4; Rom. 2:15; Rom. 3:9, 19; Eph. 2:3; Gal. 3:10; Rom. 6:23; Eph. 4:18; Rom. 8:20; Lam. 3:39; Matt. 25:41; 2 Thess. 1:9.

Chapter 7:
Of God's Covenant with Man

7.1. The distance between God and the creature is so great, that although reasonable creatures do owe obedience unto Him as their Creator, yet they could never have any fruition of Him as their blessedness and reward, but by some voluntary condescension on God's part, which He hath been pleased to express by way of covenant.
Isa. 40:13-17; Job 9:32-33; 1 Sam. 2:25; Ps. 113:5-6; Ps. 100:2-3; Job 22:2-3; Job 35:7-8; Luke 17:10; Acts 17:24-25.

7.2. The first covenant made with man was a covenant of works, wherein life was promised to Adam, and in him to his posterity, upon condition of perfect and personal obedience.
Gal. 3:12; Rom. 10:5; Rom. 5:12-20; Gen. 2:17; Gal. 3:10.

7.3. Man by his fall, having made himself incapable of life by that covenant, the Lord was pleased to make a second, commonly called the covenant of grace; wherein He freely offereth unto sinners life and salvation by Jesus Christ, requiring of them faith in Him that they may be saved, and promising to give unto all those that are ordained unto life His Holy Spirit, to make them willing and able to believe.

Gal. 3:21; Rom. 8:3; Rom. 3:20-21; Gen. 3:15; Isa. 42:6; Mark 16:15-16; John 3:16; Rom. 10:6, 9; Gal. 3:11; Ezek. 36:26-27; John 6:44-45.

7.4. This covenant of grace is frequently set forth in Scripture by the name of a Testament, in reference to the death of Jesus Christ the Testator, and to the everlasting inheritance, with all things belonging to it, therein bequeathed.
Heb. 9:15-17; Heb. 7:22; Luke 22:20; 1 Cor. 11:25.

7.5. This covenant was differently administered in the time of the law, and in the time of the gospel: under the law, it was administered by promises, prophecies, sacrifices, circumcision, the paschal lamb, and other types and ordinances delivered to the people of the Jews, all fore-signifying Christ to come: which were, for that time, sufficient and efficacious, through the operation of the Spirit, to instruct and build up the elect in faith in the promised Messiah, by whom they had full remission of sins, and eternal salvation; and is called, the Old Testament.
2 Cor. 3:6-9; Heb. 8—10; Rom. 4:11; Col. 2:11-12; 1 Cor. 5:7; 1 Cor. 10:1-4; Heb. 11:13; John 8:56; Gal. 3:7-9, 14.

7.6. Under the gospel, when Christ, the substance, was exhibited, the ordinances in which this covenant is dispensed are the preaching of the Word, and the administration of the sacraments of Baptism and the Lord's Supper: which, though fewer in number, and administered with more simplicity, and less outward glory; yet, in them, it is held forth in more fulness, evidence, and spiritual efficacy, to all nations, both Jews and Gentiles; and is called the New Testament. There are not therefore two covenants of grace, differing in substance, but one and the same, under various dispensations.

Col. 2:17; Matt. 28:19-20; 1 Cor. 11:23-25; Heb. 12:22-28; Jer. 31:33-34; Matt. 28:19; Eph. 2:15-19; Luke 22:20; Gal.3:14, 16; Rom. 3:21-23, 30; Ps. 32:1 with Rom. 4:3, 6, 16-17, 23-24; Heb. 13:8; Acts 15:11.

Chapter 8:
Of Christ the Mediator

8.1. It pleased God, in His eternal purpose, to choose and ordain the Lord Jesus, His only begotten Son, to be the Mediator between God and man; the Prophet, Priest, and King, the Head and Saviour of His Church, the Heir of all things, and Judge of the world: unto whom He did from all eternity give a people, to be His seed, and to be by Him in time redeemed, called, justified, sanctified, and glorified.
Isa. 42:1; 1 Pet. 1:19-20; John 3:16; 1 Tim. 2:5; Acts 3:22; Heb. 5:5-6; Ps. 2:6; Luke 1:33; Eph. 5:23; Heb. 1:2; Acts 17:31; John 17:6; Ps. 22:30; Isa. 53:10; 1 Tim. 2:6; Isa. 55:4-5; 1 Cor. 1:30.

8.2. The Son of God, the second person in the Trinity, being very and eternal God, of one substance and equal with the Father, did, when the fulness of time was come, take upon Him man's nature, with all the essential properties and common infirmities thereof, yet without sin; being conceived by the power of the Holy Ghost, in the womb of the virgin Mary, of her substance. So that two whole, perfect, and distinct natures, the Godhead and the manhood, were inseparably joined together in one person, without conversion, compostition, or confusion. Which person is very God, and very man, yet one Christ, the only Mediator between God and man.
John 1:1, 14; 1 John 5:20; Phil. 2:6; Gal. 4:4; Heb 2:14, 16-17; Heb. 4:15; Luke 1:27, 31, 35; Gal 4:4; Luke 1:35; Col. 2:9; Rom. 9:5; 1 Pet. 3:18; 1 Tim. 3:16; Rom. 1:3-4; 1 Tim. 2:5.

8.3. The Lord Jesus, in His human nature thus united to the divine, was sanctified and anointed with the Holy Spirit, above measure, having in Him all the treasures of wisdom and knowledge; in whom it pleased the Father that all fulness should dwell; to the end that, being holy, harmless, undefiled, and full of grace and truth, He might be thoroughly furnished to execute the office of a Mediator and Surety. Which office He took not unto Himself, but was thereunto called by His Father, who put all power and judgment into His hand, and gave Him commandment to execute the same.

Ps. 45:7; John 3:34; Col. 2:3; Col. 1:19; Heb. 7:26; John 1:14; Acts 10:38; Heb. 12:24; Heb. 7:22; Heb. 5:4-5; John 5:22, 27; Matt. 28:18; Acts 2:36.

8.4. This office the Lord Jesus did most willingly undertake; which that He might discharge, He was made under the law, and did perfectly fulfil it, endured most grievous torments immediately in His soul, and most painful sufferings in His body; was crucified, and died; was buried, and remained under the power of death; yet saw no corruption. On the third day He arose from the dead, with the same body in which He suffered, with which also He ascended into heaven, and there sitteth at the right hand of His Father, making intercession, and shall return to judge men and angels at the end of the world.

Ps. 40:7-8 with Heb. 10:5-10; John 10:18; Phil. 2:8; Gal. 4:4; Matt. 3:15; Matt. 5:17; Matt. 26:37-38; Luke 22:44; Matt. 27:46; Matt. 26—27; Phil. 2:8; Acts 2:23-24, 27; Acts 13:37; Rom. 6:9; 1 Cor. 15:3-4; John 20:25, 27; Mark 16:19; Rom. 8:34; Heb. 9:24; Heb. 7:25; Rom. 14:9-10; Acts 1:11; Acts 10:42; Matt. 13:40-42; Jude 6; 2 Pet. 2:4.

8.5. The Lord Jesus, by His perfect obedience, and sacrifice of Himself, which He, through the eternal Spirit, once offered up unto God, hath fully satisfied the justice of His Father; and purchased, not only reconciliation, but an everlasting inheritance in the kingdom of heaven, for all those whom the Father hath given unto Him.
Rom. 5:19; Heb. 9:14, 16; Heb 10:14; Eph. 5:2; Rom. 3:25-26; Dan. 9:24, 26; Col. 1:19-20; Eph. 1:11, 14; John 17:2; Heb. 9:12, 15.

8.6. Although the work of redemption was not actually wrought by Christ till after His incarnation, yet the virtue, efficacy, and benefits thereof were communicated unto the elect in all ages successively from the beginning of the world, in and by those promises, types, and sacrifices, wherein He was revealed, and signified to be the seed of the woman which should bruise the serpent's head; and the Lamb slain from the beginning of the world: being yesterday and today the same, and for ever.
Gal. 4:4-5; Gen. 3:15; Rev. 13:8; Heb. 13:8.

8.7. Christ, in the work of mediation, acteth according to both natures, by each nature doing that which is proper to itself: yet, by reason of the unity of the person, that which is proper to one nature, is sometimes in Scripture attributed to the person denominated by the other nature.
Heb. 9:14; 1 Pet. 3:18; Acts 20:28; John 3:13; 1 John 3:16.

8.8. To all those for whom Christ hath purchased redemption, He doth certainly and effectually apply and communicate the same, making intercession for them, and revealing unto them, in and by the Word, the mysteries of salvation, effectually persuading them by His Spirit to believe and obey, and governing their hearts by His Word and Spirit, overcoming all their enemies by His almighty power and wisdom, in such manner, and ways, as are most consonant to His wonderful and unsearchable dispensation.

John 6:37, 39; John 10:15-16; 1 John 2:1-2; Rom. 8:34; John 15:13, 15; Eph. 1:7-9; John 17:6; John 14:26; Heb. 12:2; 2 Cor. 4:13; Rom. 8:9, 14; Rom. 15:18-19; John 17:17; Ps. 110:1; 1 Cor. 15:25-26; Mal. 4:2-3; Col. 2:15.

Chapter 9:
Of Free Will

9.1. God hath endued the will of man with that natural liberty, that it is neither forced, nor by any absolute necessity of nature determined to good or evil.
Matt. 17:12; Jas. 1:14; Deut. 30:19.

9.2. Man, in his state of innocency, had freedom and power to will and to do that which was good, and well pleasing to God; but yet mutably, so that he might fall from it.
Eccl. 7:29; Gen. 1:26; Gen. 2:16-17; Gen. 3:6.

9.3. Man, by his fall into a state of sin, hath wholly lost all ability of will to any spiritual good accompanying salvation: so as, a natural man, being altogether averse from that good, and dead in sin, is not able, by his own strength, to convert himself, or to prepare himself thereunto.
Rom. 5:6; Rom. 8:7; John 15:5; Rom. 3:10, 12; Eph. 2:1, 5; Col. 2:13; John 6:44, 65; Eph. 2:2-5; 1 Cor. 2:14; Titus 3:3-5.

9.4. When God converts a sinner, and translates him into the state of grace, He freeth him from his natural bondage under sin; and, by His grace alone, enables him freely to will and to do that which is spiritually good; yet so, as that by reason of his remaining corruption, he doth not perfectly, nor only, will that which is good, but doth also will that which is evil.
Col. 1:13; John 8:34, 36; Phil. 2:13; Rom. 6:18, 22; Gal. 5:17; Rom. 7:15, 18-19, 21, 23.

9.5. The will of man is made perfectly and immutably free to good alone, in the state of glory only.
Eph. 4:13; Heb. 12:23; 1 John 3:2; Jude 24.

Chapter 10:
Of Effectual Calling

10.1. All those whom God hath predestinated unto life, and those only, He is pleased in His appointed and accepted time effectually to call, by His Word and Spirit, out of that state of sin and death, in which they are by nature, to grace and salvation by Jesus Christ; enlightening their minds spiritually and savingly to understand the things of God; taking away their heart of stone, and giving unto them a heart of flesh; renewing their wills, and by His almighty power determining them to that which is good, and effectually drawing them to Jesus Christ: yet so, as they come most freely, being made willing by His grace.
Rom. 8:30; Rom. 11:7; Eph. 1:10-11; 2 Thess. 2:13-14; 2 Cor. 3:3, 6; Rom. 8:2; Eph. 2:1-5; 2 Tim. 1:9-10; Acts 26:18; 1 Cor. 2:10, 12; Eph. 1:17-18; Ezek. 36:26; Ezek. 11:19; Phil. 2:13; Deut. 30:6; Ezek. 36:27; Eph. 1:19; John 6:44-45; Song of Sol. 1:4; Ps. 110:3; John 6:37; Rom. 6:16-18.

10.2. This effectual call is of God's free and special grace alone, not from anything at all foreseen in man, who is altogether passive therein, until being quickened and renewed by the Holy Spirit, he is thereby enabled to answer this call, and to embrace the grace offered and conveyed in it.
2 Tim. 1:9; Titus 3:4-5; Eph. 2:4-5, 8-9; Rom. 9:11; 1 Cor. 2:14; Rom. 8:7; Eph. 2:5; John 6:37; Ezek. 36:27; John 5:25.

10.3. Elect infants, dying in infancy, are regenerated, and saved by Christ through the Spirit, who worketh when, and where, and how He pleaseth: so also, are all other elect persons who are uncapable of being outwardly called by the ministry of the Word.
Luke 18:15-16, and Acts 2:38-39, and John 3:3, 5, and 1 John 5:12, and Rom. 8:9 compared; John 3:8; 1 John 5:12; Acts 4:12.

10.4. Others, not elected, although they may be called by the ministry of the Word, and may have some common operations of the Spirit, yet they never truly come unto Christ, and therefore cannot be saved: much less can men, not professing the Christian religion, be saved in any other way whatsoever, be they never so diligent to frame their lives according to the light of nature, and the law of that religion they do profess. And, to assert and maintain that they may, is very pernicious, and to be detested.
Matt. 22:14; Matt. 7:22; Matt. 13:20-21; Heb. 6:4-5; John 6:64-66; John 8:24; Acts 4:12; John 14:6; Eph. 2:12; John 4:22; John 17:3; 2 John 9-11; 1 Cor. 16:22; Gal. 1:6-8.

Chapter 11:
Of Justification

11.1. Those whom God effectually calleth, He also freely justifieth: not by infusing righteousness into them, but by pardoning their sins, and by accounting and accepting their persons as righteous, not for anything wrought in them, or done by them, but for Christ's sake alone; nor by imputing faith itself, the act of believing, or any other evangelical obedience to them, as their righteousness, but by imputing the obedience and satisfaction of Christ unto them, they receiving and resting on Him and His righteousness by faith; which faith they have not of themselves, it is the gift of God.
Rom. 8:30; Rom. 3:24; Rom. 4:5-8; 2 Cor. 5:19, 21; Rom. 3:22, 24-25, 27-28; Titus 3:5, 7; Eph. 1:7; Jer. 23:6; 1 Cor. 1:30-31; Rom. 5:17-19; Acts 10:43; Gal. 2:16; Phil. 3:9; Acts 13:38-39; Eph. 2:7-8.

11.2. Faith, thus receiving and resting on Christ, and His righteousness, is the alone instrument of justification; yet it is not alone in the person justified, but is ever accompanied with all other saving graces, and is no dead faith, but worketh by love.
John 1:12; Rom. 3:28; Rom. 5:1; Jas. 2:17, 22, 26; Gal. 5:6.

11.3. Christ, by His obedience and death, did fully discharge the debt of all those that are thus justified, and did make a proper, real, and full satisfaction to His Father's justice in their behalf. Yet, inasmuch as He was given by the Father for them; and His obedience and satisfaction accepted in their stead; and both freely, not for anything in them; their justification is only of free grace; that both the exact justice, and rich grace of God, might be glorified in the justification of sinners.

Rom. 5:8-10, 19; 1 Tim. 2:5-6; Heb. 10:10, 14; Dan. 9:24, 26; Isa. 53:4-6, 10-12; Rom. 8:32; 2 Cor. 5:21; Matt. 3:17; Eph. 5:2; Rom. 3:24; Eph. 1:7; Rom. 3:26; Eph. 2:7.

Westminster Confession of Faith

11.4. God did, from all eternity, decree to justify all the elect, and Christ did, in the fulness of time, die for their sins, and rise again for their justification: nevertheless, they are not justified, until the Holy Spirit doth, in due time, actually apply Christ unto them.
Gal. 3:8; 1 Pet. 1:2, 19-20; Rom. 8:30; Gal. 4:4; 1 Tim. 2:6; Rom. 4:25; Col. 1:21-22; Gal 2:16; Titus 3:3-7.

11.5. God doth continue to forgive the sins of those that are justified; and, although they can never fall from the state of justification; yet they may, by their sins, fall under God's fatherly displeasure, and not have the light of His countenance restored unto them, until they humble themselves, confess their sins, beg pardon, and renew their faith and repentance.
Matt. 6:12; 1 John 1:7, 9; 1 John 2:1-2; Luke 22:32; John 10:28; Heb. 10:14; Ps. 89:31-33; Ps. 51:7-12; Ps. 32:5; Matt. 26:75; 1 Cor. 11:30, 32; Luke 1:20.

11.6. The justification of believers under the old testament was, in all these respects, one and the same with the justification of believers under the new testament.
Gal. 3:9, 13-14; Rom. 4:22-24; Heb. 13:8.

Chapter 12:
Of Adoption

12.1. All those that are justified, God vouchsafeth, in and for His only Son Jesus Christ, to make partakers of the grace of adoption: by which they are taken into the number, and enjoy the liberties and privileges of the children of God, have His name put upon them, receive the spirit of adoption, have access to the throne of grace with boldness, are enabled to cry, Abba, Father, are pitied, protected, provided for, and chastened by Him as by a father; yet never cast off, but sealed to the day of redemption, and inherit the promises, as heirs of everlasting salvation.
Eph. 1:5; Gal. 4:4-5; Rom. 8:17; John 1:12; Jer. 14:9; 2 Cor. 6:18; Rev. 3:12; Rom. 8:15; Eph. 3:12; Rom. 5:2; Gal. 4:6; Ps. 103:13; Prov. 14:26; Matt. 6:30, 32; 1 Pet. 5:7; Heb. 12:6; Lam. 3:31; Eph. 4:30; Heb. 6:12; 1 Pet. 1:3-4; Heb. 1:14.

Chapter 13:
Of Sanctification

13.1. They who are effectually called and regenerated, having a new heart and a new spirit created in them, are further sanctified, really and personally, through the virtue of Christ's death and resurrection, by His Word and Spirit dwelling in them: the dominion of the whole body of sin is destroyed, and the several lusts thereof are more and more weakened and mortified; and they more and more quickened and strengthened in all saving graces, to the practice of true holiness, without which no man shall see the Lord.
1 Cor. 6:11; Acts 20:32; Phil. 3:10; Rom. 6:5-6; John 17:17; Eph. 5:26; 2 Thess. 2:13; Rom. 6:6, 14; Gal. 5:24; Rom. 8:13; Col. 1:11; Eph. 3:16-19; 2 Cor. 7:1; Heb. 12:14.

13.2. This sanctification is throughout, in the whole man; yet imperfect in this life, there abiding still some remnants of corruption in every part: whence ariseth a continual and irreconcilable war; the flesh lusting against the Spirit, and the Spirit against the flesh.
1 Thess. 5:23; 1 John 1:10; Rom. 7:18, 23; Phil. 3:12; Gal. 5:17; 1 Pet. 2:11.

13.3. In which war, although the remaining corruption, for a time, may much prevail; yet through the continual supply of strength from the sanctifying Spirit of Christ, the regenerate part doth overcome; and so, the saints grow in grace, perfecting holiness in the fear of God.
Rom. 7:23; Rom. 6:14; 1 John 5:4; Eph. 4:15-16; 2 Pet. 3:18; 2 Cor. 3:18; 2 Cor. 7:1.

Chapter 14:
Of Saving Faith

14.1. The grace of faith, whereby the elect are enabled to believe to the saving of their souls, is the work of the Spirit of Christ in their hearts; and is ordinarily wrought by the ministry of the Word: by which also, and by the administration of the sacraments, and prayer, it is increased and strengthened.
Heb. 10:39; 2 Cor. 4:13; Eph. 1:17-19; Eph. 2:8; Rom. 10:14, 17; 1 Pet. 2:2; Acts 20:32; Rom. 4:11; Luke 17:5; Rom. 1:16-17.

14.2. By this faith, a Christian believeth to be true whatsoever is revealed in the Word, for the authority of God Himself speaking therein; and acteth differently upon that which each particular passage thereof containeth; yielding obedience to the commands, trembling at the threatenings, and embracing the promises of God for this life, and that which is to come. But the principal acts of saving faith are accepting, receiving, and resting upon Christ alone for justification, sanctification, and eternal life, by virtue of the covenant of grace.

John 4:42; 1 Thess. 2:13; 1 John 5:10; Acts 24:14; Rom. 16:26; Isa. 66:2; Heb. 11:13; 1 Tim. 4:8; John 1:12; Acts 16:31; Gal. 2:20; Acts 15:11.

14.3. This faith is different in degrees, weak or strong; may be often and many ways assailed, and weakened, but gets the victory; growing up in many to the attainment of a full assurance through Christ, who is both the author and finisher of our faith.
Heb. 5:13-14; Rom. 4:19-20; Matt. 6:30; Matt. 8:10; Luke 22:31-32; Eph. 6:16; 1 John 5:4-5; Heb. 6:11-12; Heb. 10:22; Col. 2:2; Heb. 12:2.

Chapter 15:
Of Repentance Unto Life

15.1. Repentance unto life is an evangelical grace, the doctrine whereof is to be preached by every minister of the Gospel, as well as that of faith in Christ.
Zech. 12:10; Acts 11:18; Luke 24:47; Mark 1:5; Acts 20:21.

15.2. By it, a sinner, out of the sight and sense not only of the danger, but also of the filthiness and odiousness of his sins, as contrary to the holy nature and righteous law of God; and upon the apprehension of His mercy in Christ to such as are penitent, so grieves for, and hates his sins, as to turn from them all unto God, purposing and endeavoring to walk with Him in all the ways of His commandments.
Ezek. 18:30-31; Ezek. 36:31; Isa. 30:22; Ps. 51:4; Jer. 31:18-19; Joel 2:12-13; Amos 5:15; Ps. 119:128; 2 Cor. 7:11; Ps. 119:6, 59, 106; Luke 1:6; 2 Kings 23:25.

15.3. Although repentance be not to be rested in, as any satisfaction for sin, or any cause of the pardon thereof, which is the act of God's free grace in Christ; yet is it of such necessity to all sinners, that none may expect pardon without it.
Ezek. 36:31-32; Ezek. 16:61-63; Hos. 14:2, 4; Rom. 3:24; Eph. 1:7; Luke 13:3, 5; Acts 17:30-31.

15.4. As there is no sin so small, but it deserves damnation, so there is no sin so great, that it can bring damnation upon those who truly repent.
Rom. 6:23; Rom. 5:12; Matt. 12:36; Isa. 55:7; Rom. 8:1; Isa. 1:16, 18.

15.5. Men ought not to content themselves with a general repentance, but it is every man's duty to endeavour to repent of his particular sins, particularly.
Ps. 19:13; Luke 19:8; 1 Tim. 1:13, 15.

15.6. As every man is bound to make private confession of his sins to God, praying for the pardon thereof; upon which, and the forsaking of them, he shall find mercy; so, he that scandalizeth his brother, or the Church of Christ, ought to be willing, by a private or public confession, and sorrow for his sin, to declare his repentance to those that are offended, who are thereupon to be reconciled to him, and in love to receive him.
Ps. 51:4-5, 7, 9, 14; Ps. 32:5-6; Prov. 28:13; 1 John 1:9; Jas. 5:16; Luke 17:3-4; Josh. 7:19; Ps. 51; 2 Cor. 2:8.

Chapter 16:
Of Good Works

16.1. Good works are only such as God hath commanded in His holy Word, and not such as, without the warrant thereof, are devised by men, out of blind zeal, or upon any pretence of good intention.

Mic. 6:8; Rom. 12:2; Heb. 13:21; Matt. 15:9; Isa. 29:13; 1 Pet. 1:18; Rom. 10:2; John 16:2; 1 Sam. 15:21-23.

16.2. These good works, done in obedience to God's commandments, are the fruits and evidences of a true and lively faith: and by them believers manifest their thankfulness, strengthen their assurance, edify their brethren, adorn the profession of the Gospel, stop the mouths of the adversaries, and glorify God, whose workmanship they are, created in Christ Jesus thereunto; that, having their fruit unto holiness, they may have the end, eternal life.
Jas. 2:18, 22; Ps. 116:12-13; 1 Pet. 2:9; 1 John 2:3, 5; 2 Pet. 1:5-10; 2 Cor. 9:2; Matt. 5:16; Titus 2:5, 9-12; 1 Tim. 6:1; 1 Pet. 2:15; 1 Pet. 2:12; Phil. 1:11; John 15:8; Eph. 2:10; Rom. 6:22.

16.3. Their ability to do good works is not at all of themselves, but wholly from the Spirit of Christ. And that they may be enabled thereunto, besides the graces they have already received, there is required an actual influence of the same Holy Spirit, to work in them to will and to do of His good pleasure: yet are they not hereupon to grow negligent, as if they were not bound to perform any duty, unless upon a special motion of the Spirit; but they ought to be diligent in stirring up the grace of God that is in them. *John 15:4-5; Ezek. 36:26-27; Phil. 2:13; Phil. 4:13; 2 Cor. 3:5; Phil. 2:12; Heb. 6:11-12; 2 Pet. 1:3, 5, 10-11; Isa. 64:7; 2 Tim. 1:6; Acts 26:6-7; Jude 1:20-21.*

Westminster Confession of Faith

16.4. They, who in their obedience attain to the greatest height which is possible in this life, are so far from being able to supererogate, and to do more than God requires, as that they fall short of much which in duty they are bound to do.
Luke 17:10; Neh. 13:22; Job 9:2-3; Gal. 5:17.

16.5. We cannot, by our best works, merit pardon of sin, or eternal life at the hand of God, by reason of the great disproportion that is between them and the glory to come; and the infinite distance that is between us and God, whom, by them, we can neither profit, nor satisfy for the debt of our former sins, but when we have done all we can, we have done but our duty, and are unprofitable servants; and because, as they are good, they proceed from His Spirit; and as they are wrought by us, they are defiled, and mixed with so much weakness and imperfection, that they cannot endure the severity of God's judgment.

Rom. 3:20; Rom. 4:2, 4, 6; Eph. 2:8-9; Titus 3:5-7; Rom. 8:18; Ps. 16:2; Job 22:2-3; Job 35:7-8; Luke 17:10; Gal. 5:22-23; Isa. 64:6; Gal. 5:17; Rom. 7:15, 18; Ps. 143:2; Ps. 130:3.

16.6. Yet notwithstanding, the persons of believers being accepted through Christ, their good works also are accepted in Him, not as though they were in this life wholly unblameable and unreprovable in God's sight; but that He, looking upon them in His Son, is pleased to accept and reward that which is sincere, although accompanied with many weaknesses and imperfections.
Eph. 1:6; 1 Pet. 2:5; Ex. 28:38; Gen. 4:4 with Heb. 11:4; Job 9:20; Ps. 143:2; Heb. 13:20-21; 2 Cor. 8:12; Heb. 6:10; Matt. 25:21, 23.

Westminster Confession of Faith

16.7. Works done by unregenerate men, although, for the matter of them, they may be things which God commands, and of good use both to themselves and others: yet, because they proceed not from a heart purified by faith; nor are done in a right manner according to the Word; nor to a right end, the glory of God; they are therefore sinful, and cannot please God, or make a man meet to receive grace from God. And yet, their neglect of them is more sinful, and displeasing unto God.
2 Kings 10:30-31; 1 Kings 21:27, 29; Phil. 1:15-16, 18; Gen. 4:5 with Heb. 11:4, 6; 1 Cor. 13:3; Isa. 1:12; Matt. 6:2, 5, 16; Hag. 2:14; Titus 1:15; Amos 5:21-22; Hos. 1:4; Rom. 9:16; Titus 3:5; Ps. 14:4; Ps. 36:3; Job 21:14-15; Matt. 25:41-43, 45; Matt. 23:23.

Chapter 17:
Of the Perseverance of the Saints

17.1. They, whom God hath accepted in His Beloved, effectually called, and sanctified by His Spirit, can neither totally, nor finally, fall away from the state of grace: but shall certainly persevere therein to the end, and be eternally saved.
Phil. 1:6; 2 Pet. 1:10; John 10:28-29; 1 John 3:9; 1 Pet. 1:5, 9.

17.2. This perseverance of the saints depends not upon their own free will, but upon the immutability of the decree of election, flowing from the free and unchangeable love of God the Father; upon the efficacy of the merit and intercession of Jesus Christ; the abiding of the Spirit, and of the seed of God within them; and the nature of the covenant of grace; from all which ariseth also the certainty and infallibility thereof.

2 Tim. 2:18-19; Jer. 31:3; Heb. 10:10, 14; Heb. 13:20-21; Heb. 9:12-15; Rom. 8:33-39; John 17:11, 24; Luke 22:32; Heb. 7:25; John 14:16-17; 1 John 2:27; 1 John 3:9; Jer. 32:40; John 10:28; 2 Thess. 3:3; 1 John 2:19.

17.3. Nevertheless, they may, through the temptations of Satan and of the world, the prevalency of corruption remaining in them, and the neglect of the means of their preservation, fall into grievous sins; and, for a time, continue therein: whereby they incur God's displeasure, and grieve His Holy Spirit, come to be deprived of some measure of their graces and comforts, have their hearts hardened, and their consciences wounded, hurt and scandalize others, and bring temporal judgments upon themselves.

Matt. 26:70, 72, 74; Ps. 51:title and vs. 14; Isa. 64:5, 7, 9; 2 Sam. 11:27; Eph. 4:30; Ps. 51:8, 10, 12; Rev. 2:4; Song of Sol. 5:2-4, 6; Isa. 63:17; Mark 6:52; Mark 16:14; Ps. 32:3-4; Ps. 51:8; 2 Sam. 12:14; Ps. 89:31-32; 1 Cor. 11:32.

Chapter 18:
Of the Assurance of Grace and Salvation

18.1. Although hypocrites and other unregenerate men may vainly deceive themselves with false hopes, and carnal presumptions of being in the favour of God, and estate of salvation; which hope of theirs shall perish: yet such as truly believe in the Lord Jesus, and love Him in sincerity, endeavouring to walk in all good conscience before Him, may, in this life, be certainly assured that they are in the state of grace, and may rejoice in the hope of the glory of God, which hope shall never make them ashamed.
Job 8:13-14; Mic. 3:11; Deut. 29:19; John 8:41; Matt. 7:22-23; 1 John 2:3; 1 John 3:14, 18-19, 21, 24; 1 John 5:13; Rom. 5:2, 5.

18.2. This certainty is not a bare conjectural and probable persuasion, grounded upon a fallible hope; but an infallible assurance of faith, founded upon the divine truth of the promises of salvation, the inward evidence of those graces unto which these promises are made, the testimony of the Spirit of adoption witnessing with our spirits that we are the children of God: which Spirit is the earnest of our inheritance, whereby we are sealed to the day of redemption.
Heb. 6:11, 19; Heb. 6:17-18; 2 Pet. 1:4-5, 10-11; 1 John 2:3; 1 John 3:14; 2 Cor. 1:12; Rom. 8:15-16; Eph. 1:13-14; Eph. 4:30; 2 Cor. 1:21-22.

18.3. This infallible assurance doth not so belong to the essence of faith, but that a true believer may wait long, and conflict with many difficulties before he be partaker of it: yet, being enabled by the Spirit to know the things which are freely given him of God, he may without extraordinary revelation, in the right use of ordinary means, attain thereunto. And therefore it is the duty of everyone to give all diligence to make his calling and election sure; that thereby his heart may be enlarged in peace and joy in the Holy Ghost, in love and thankfulness to God, and in strength and cheerfulness in the duties of obedience, the proper fruits of this assurance; so far is it from inclining men to looseness.
1 John 5:13; Isa. 50:10; Mark 9:24; Ps. 88; Ps. 77:1-12; 1 Cor. 2:12; 1 John 4:13; Heb. 6:11-12; Eph. 3:17-19; 2 Pet. 1:10; Rom. 5:1-2, 5; Rom. 14:17; Rom. 15:13; Eph. 1:3-4; Ps. 4:6-7; Ps. 119:32; 1 John 2:1-2; Rom. 6:1-2; Titus 2:11-12, 14; 2 Cor. 7:1; Rom. 8:1, 12; 1 John 3:2-3; Ps. 130:4; 1 John 1:6-7.

18.4. True believers may have the assurance of their salvation divers ways shaken, diminished, and intermitted; as, by negligence in preserving of it, by falling into some special sin, which woundeth the conscience and grieveth the Spirit; by some sudden or vehement temptation, by God's withdrawing the light of His countenance, and suffering even such as fear Him to walk in darkness and to have no light: yet are they never utterly destitute of that seed of God, and life of faith, that love of Christ and the brethren, that sincerity of heart, and conscience of duty, out of which, by the operation of the Spirit, this assurance may, in due time, be revived; and by the which, in the mean time, they are supported from utter despair.
Song of Sol. 5:2-3, 6; Ps. 51:8, 12, 14; Eph. 4:30-31; Ps. 77:1-10; Matt. 26:69-72; Ps. 31:22; Ps. 88; Isa. 50:10; 1 John 3:9; Luke 22:32; Job 13:15; Ps. 73:15; Ps. 51:8, 12; Isa. 50:10; Mic. 7:7-9; Jer. 32:40; Isa. 54:7-10; Ps. 22:1; Ps. 88.

Chapter 19:
Of the Law of God

19.1. God gave to Adam a law, as a covenant of works, by which He bound him and all his posterity to personal, entire, exact, and perpetual obedience; promised life upon the fulfilling, and threatened death upon the breach of it: and endued him with power and ability to keep it.
Gen. 1:26-27 with Gen. 2:17; Rom. 2:14-15; Rom. 10:5; Rom. 5:12, 19; Gal. 3:10, 12; Eccl. 7:29; Job 28:28.

19.2. This law, after his fall, continued to be a perfect rule of righteousness, and, as such, was delivered by God upon Mount Sinai, in ten commandments, and written in two tables: the four first commandments containing our duty towards God; and the other six our duty to man.
Jas. 1:25; Jas. 2:8, 10-12; Rom. 13:8-9; Deut. 5:32; Deut. 10:4; Ex. 34:1; Matt. 22:37-40.

19.3. Beside this law, commonly called moral, God was pleased to give to the people of Israel, as a church under age, ceremonial laws, containing several typical ordinances, partly of worship, prefiguring Christ, His graces, actions, sufferings, and benefits; and partly holding forth divers instructions of moral duties. All which ceremonial laws are now abrogated, under the New Testament.
Heb. 9; Heb. 10:1; Gal. 4:1-3; Col. 2:17; 1 Cor. 5:7; 2 Cor. 6:17; Jude 1:23; Col. 2:14, 16-17; Dan. 9:27; Eph. 2:15-16.

19.4. To them also, as a body politic, He gave sundry judicial laws, which expired together with the State of that people; not obliging any other now, further than the general equity thereof may require.
Ex. 21; Ex. 22:1-29; Gen. 49:10 with 1 Pet. 2:13-14; Matt. 5:17, 38-39; 1 Cor. 9:8-10.

19.5. The moral law doth for ever bind all, as well justified persons as others, to the obedience thereof; and that, not only in regard of the matter contained in it, but also in respect of the authority of God the Creator, who gave it: neither doth Christ, in the Gospel, any way dissolve, but much strengthen this obligation.
Rom. 13:8-10; Eph. 6:2; 1 John 2:3-4, 7-8; Jas. 2:10-11; Matt. 5:17-19; Jas. 2:8; Rom. 3:31.

19.6. Although true believers be not under the law, as a covenant of works, to be thereby justified or condemned; yet is it of great use to them, as well as to others; in that, as a rule of life informing them of the will of God, and their duty, it directs, and binds them to walk accordingly; discovering also the sinful pollutions of their nature, hearts, and lives; so as, examining themselves thereby, they may come to further conviction of, humiliation for, and hatred against sin; together with a clearer sight of the need they have of Christ, and the perfection of His obedience. It is likewise of use to the regenerate, to restrain their corruptions, in that it forbids sin; and the threatenings of it serve to show what even their sins deserve; and what afflictions, in this life, they may expect for them, although freed from the curse thereof threatened in the law. The promises of it, in like manner, show them God's approbation of obedience, and what blessings they may expect upon the performance thereof; although not as due to them by the law, as a covenant of works. So as, a man's doing good, and refraining from evil, because the law encourageth to the one, and deterreth from the other, is no evidence of his being under the law; and not under grace.

Rom. 6:14; Gal. 2:16; Gal. 3:13; Gal. 4:4-5; Acts 13:39; Rom. 8:1; Rom. 7:12, 22, 25; Ps. 119:4-6; 1 Cor. 7:19; Gal. 5:14, 16, 18-23; Rom. 7:7; Rom. 3:20; Jas. 1:23-25; Rom. 7:9, 14, 24; Gal. 3:24; Rom. 7:24-25; Rom. 8:3-4; Jas. 2:11; Ps. 119:101, 104, 128; Ezra 9:13-14; Ps. 89:30-34; Lev. 26:1-14 with 2 Cor. 6:16; Eph. 6:2-3; Ps. 37:11 with Matt. 5:5; Ps. 19:11; Gal. 2:16; Luke 17:10; Rom. 6:12, 14; 1 Pet. 3:8-12 with Ps. 34:12-16; Heb. 12:28-29.

19.7. Neither are the forementioned uses of the law contrary to the grace of the Gospel, but do sweetly comply with it; the Spirit of Christ subduing and enabling the will of man to do that, freely and cheerfully, which the will of God, revealed in the law, requireth to be done.
Gal. 3:21; Ezek. 36:27; Heb. 8:10 with Jer. 31:33.

Chapter 20:
Of Christian Liberty, and Liberty of Conscience

20.1. The liberty which Christ hath purchased for believers under the Gospel consists in their freedom from the guilt of sin, the condemning wrath of God, the curse of the moral law; and, in their being delivered from this present evil world, bondage to Satan, and dominion of sin; from the evil of afflictions, the sting of death, the victory of the grave, and everlasting damnation; as also, in their free access to God, and their yielding obedience unto Him, not out of slavish fear, but a child-like love and willing mind. All which were common also to believers under the law. But, under the new testament, the liberty of Christians is further enlarged, in their freedom from the yoke of the ceremonial law, to which the Jewish Church was subjected; and in greater boldness of access to the throne of grace, and in fuller communications of the free Spirit of God, than believers under the law did ordinarily partake of.
Titus 2:14; 1 Thess. 1:10; Gal. 3:13; Gal. 1:4; Col. 1:13; Acts 26:18; Rom. 6:14; Rom. 8:28; Ps. 119:71; 1 Cor. 15:54-57; Rom. 8:1; Rom. 5:1-2; Rom. 8:14-15; 1 John 4:18; Gal. 3:9, 14; Gal. 4:1-3, 6-7; Gal. 5:1; Acts 15:10-11; Heb. 4:14, 16; Heb. 10:19-22; John 7:38-39; 2 Cor. 3:13, 17-18.

20.2. God alone is Lord of the conscience, and hath left it free from the doctrines and commandments of men, which are in any thing contrary to His Word; or beside it, if matters of faith or worship. So that, to believe such doctrines, or to obey such commands, out of conscience, is to betray true liberty of conscience: and the requiring of an implicit faith, and an absolute and blind obedience is to destroy liberty of conscience, and reason also.
Jas. 4:12; Rom. 14:4; Acts 4:19; Acts 5:29; 1 Cor. 7:23; Matt. 23:8-10; 2 Cor. 1:24; Matt. 15:9; Col. 2:20, 22-23; Gal. 1:10; Gal. 2:4-5; Gal. 5:1; Rom. 10:17; Rom. 14:23; Isa. 8:20; Acts 17:11; John 4:22; Hos. 5:11; Rev. 13:12, 16-17; Jer. 8:9.

20.3. They who, upon pretence of Christian liberty, do practice any sin, or cherish any lust, do thereby destroy the end of Christian liberty, which is, that being delivered out of the hands of our enemies, we might serve the Lord without fear, in holiness and righteousness before Him, all the days of our life.
Gal. 5:13; 1 Pet. 2:16; 2 Pet. 2:19; John 8:34; Luke 1:74-75.

20.4. And because the powers which God hath ordained, and the liberty which Christ hath purchased, are not intended by God to destroy, but mutually to uphold and preserve one another; they who, upon pretence of Christian liberty, shall oppose any lawful power, or the lawful exercise of it, whether it be civil or ecclesiastical, resist the ordinance of God. And, for their publishing of such opinions, or maintaining of such practices, as are contrary to the light of nature, or to the known principles of Christianity, whether concerning faith, worship or conversation; or, to the power of godliness; or, such erroneous opinions or practices, as either in their own nature, or in the manner of publishing or maintaining them, are destructive to the external peace and order which Christ hath established in the Church, they may lawfully be called to account, and proceeded against by the censures of the Church, and by the power of the civil magistrate.

Matt. 12:25; 1 Pet. 2:13-14, 16; Rom. 13:1-8; Heb. 13:17; Rom. 1:32 with 1 Cor. 5:1, 5, 11, 13; 2 John 10-11, and 2 Thess. 3:14, and 1 Tim. 6:3-5, and Titus 1:10-11, 13, and Titus 3:10 with Matt. 18:15-17; 1 Tim. 1:19-20; Rev. 2:2, 14-15, 20; Rev. 3:9; Deut. 13:6-12; Rom. 13:3-4 with 2 John 10-11; Ezra 7:23, 25-28; Rev. 17:12, 16-17; Neh. 13:15, 17, 21-22, 25, 30; 2 Kings 23:5-6, 9, 20-21; 2 Chron. 34:33; 2 Chron. 15:12-13, 16; Dan. 3:29; 1 Tim. 2:2; Isa. 49:23; Zech. 13:2-3.

Chapter 21:
Of Religious Worship, and the Sabbath Day

21.1. The light of nature showeth that there is a God, who hath lordship and sovereignty over all, is good, and doth good unto all, and is therefore to be feared, loved, praised, called upon, trusted in, and served, with all the heart, and with all the soul, and with all the might. But the acceptable way of worshipping the true God is instituted by Himself, and so limited by His own revealed will, that He may not be worshipped according to the imaginations and devices of men, or the suggestions of Satan, under any visible representation, or any other way not prescribed in the holy Scripture.

Rom. 1:20; Acts 17:24; Ps. 119:68; Jer. 10:7; Ps. 31:23; Ps. 18:3; Rom. 10:12; Ps. 62:8; Josh. 24:14; Mark 12:33; Deut. 12:32; Matt. 15:9; Acts 17:25; Matt. 4:9-10; Deut. 4:15-20; Ex. 20:4-6; Col. 2:23.

21.2. Religious worship is to be given to God, the Father, Son, and Holy Ghost; and to Him alone; not to angels, saints, or any other creature: and since the fall, not without a Mediator; nor in the mediation of any other but of Christ alone.
Matt. 4:10 with John 5:23 and 2 Cor. 13:14; Col. 2:18; Rev. 19:10; Rom. 1:25; John 14:6; 1 Tim. 2:5; Eph. 2:18; Col. 3:17.

21.3. Prayer, with thanksgiving, being one special part of religious worship, is by God required of all men: and that it may be accepted, it is to be made in the name of the Son, by the help of His Spirit, according to His will, with understanding, reverence, humility, fervency, faith, love, and perseverance; and, if vocal, in a known tongue.
Phil. 4:6; Ps. 65:2; John 14:13-14; 1 Pet. 2:5; Rom. 8:26; 1 John 5:14; Ps. 47:7; Eccl. 5:1-2; Heb. 12:28; Gen. 18:27; Jas. 5:16; Jas. 1:6-7; Mark 11:24; Matt. 6:12, 14-15; Col. 4:2; Eph. 6:18; 1 Cor. 14:14.

21.4. Prayer is to be made for things lawful, and for all sorts of men living, or that shall live hereafter: but not for the dead, nor for those of whom it may be known that they have sinned the sin unto death.
1 John 5:14; 1 Tim. 2:1-2; John 17:20; 2 Sam. 7:29; Ruth 4:12; 2 Sam. 12:21-23 with Luke 16:25-26; Rev. 14:13; 1 John 5:16.

21.5. The reading of the Scriptures with godly fear; the sound preaching and conscionable hearing of the Word, in obedience unto God, with understanding, faith, reverence; singing of psalms with grace in the heart; as also, the due administration and worthy receiving of the sacraments instituted by Christ; are all parts of the ordinary religious worship of God: beside religious oaths, vows, solemn fastings, and thanksgivings, upon special occasions, which are, in their several times and seasons, to be used in a holy and religious manner.

Acts 15:21; Rev. 1:3; 2 Tim. 4:2; Jas. 1:22; Acts 10:33; Matt. 13:19; Heb. 4:2; Isa. 66:2; Col. 3:16; Eph. 5:19; Jas. 5:13; Matt. 28:19; 1 Cor. 11:23-29; Acts 2:42; Deut. 6:13 with Neh. 10:29; Isa. 19:21 with Eccl. 5:4-5; Joel 2:12; Esther 4:16; Matt. 9:15; 1 Cor. 7:5; Ps. 107; Esther 9:22; Heb. 12:28.

21.6. Neither prayer, nor any other part of religious worship, is now under the Gospel either tied unto, or made more acceptable by any place in which it is performed, or towards which it is directed: but God is to be worshipped everywhere, in spirit and truth; as in private families daily, and in secret each one by himself; so, more solemnly, in the public assemblies, which are not carelessly or wilfully to be neglected, or forsaken, when God, by His Word or providence, calleth thereunto.

John 4:21; Mal. 1:11; 1 Tim. 2:8; John 4:23-24; Jer. 10:25; Deut. 6:6-7; Job 1:5; 2 Sam. 6:18, 20; 1 Pet. 3:7; Acts 10:2; Matt. 6:11; Matt. 6:6; Eph. 6:18; Isa. 56:6-7; Heb. 10:25; Prov. 1:20-21, 24; Prov. 8:34; Acts 13:42; Luke 4:16; Acts 2:42.

21.7. As it is the law of nature, that, in general, a due proportion of time be set apart for the worship of God; so, in His Word, by a positive, moral, and perpetual commandment, binding all men, in all ages, He hath particularly appointed one day in seven, for a Sabbath, to be kept holy unto Him: which, from the beginning of the world to the resurrection of Christ, was the last day of the week; and, from the resurrection of Christ, was changed into the first day of the week, which, in Scripture, is called the Lord's Day, and is to be continued to the end of the world, as the Christian Sabbath.

Ex. 20:8, 10-11; Isa. 56:2, 4, 6-7; Gen. 2:2-3; 1 Cor. 16:1-2; Acts 20:7; Rev. 1:10; Ex. 20:8, 10 with Matt. 5:17-18.

21.8. This Sabbath is then kept holy unto the Lord, when men, after a due preparing of their hearts, and ordering of their common affairs beforehand, do not only observe an holy rest, all the day, from their own works, words, and thoughts about their worldly employments, and recreations, but also are taken up the whole time in the public and private exercises of His worship, and in the duties of necessity and mercy.
Ex. 20:8; Ex. 16:23, 25-26, 29-30; Ex. 31:15-17; Isa. 58:13; Neh. 13:15-19, 21-22; Isa. 58:13; Matt. 12:1-13.

Chapter 22:
Of Lawful Oaths and Vows

22.1. A lawful oath is a part of religious worship, wherein, upon just occasion, the person swearing solemnly calleth God to witness what he asserteth, or promiseth; and to judge him according to the truth or falsehood of what he sweareth.
Deut. 10:20; Ex. 20:7; Lev. 19:12; 2 Cor. 1:23; 2 Chron. 6:22-23.

22.2. The name of God only is that by which men ought to swear; and therein it is to be used with all holy fear and reverence. Therefore, to swear vainly or rashly, by that glorious and dreadful Name; or, to swear at all by any other thing, is sinful, and to be abhorred. Yet, as in matters of weight and moment, an oath is warranted by the Word of God, under the New Testament, as well as under the Old; so a lawful oath, being imposed by lawful authority, in such matters ought to be taken.
Deut. 6:13; Ex. 20:7; Jer. 5:7; Matt. 5:34, 37; Jas. 5:12; Heb. 6:16; 2 Cor. 1:23; Isa. 65:16; 1 Kings 8:31; Neh. 13:25; Ezra 10:5.

22.3. Whosoever taketh an oath ought duly to consider the weightiness of so solemn an act; and therein to avouch nothing, but what he is fully persuaded is the truth. Neither may any man bind himself by oath to anything but what is good and just, and what he believeth so to be, and what he is able and resolved to perform. Yet is it a sin to refuse an oath touching anything that is good and just, being imposed by lawful authority.
Ex. 20:7; Jer. 4:2; Gen. 24:2-3, 5-6, 8-9; Num. 5:19, 21; Neh. 5:12; Ex. 22:7-11.

22.4. An oath is to be taken in the plain and common sense of the words, without equivocation, or mental reservation. It cannot oblige to sin: but in anything not sinful, being taken, it binds to performance, although to a man's own hurt. Nor is it to be violated, although made to heretics, or infidels.
Jer. 4:2; Ps. 24:4; 1 Sam. 25:22, 32-34; Ps. 15:4; Ezek. 17:16, 18-19; Josh. 9:18-19 with 2 Sam. 21:1.

22.5. A vow is of the like nature with a promissory oath, and ought to be made with the like religious care, and to be performed with the like faithfulness.
Isa. 19:21; Eccl. 5:4-6; Ps. 61:8; Ps. 66:13-14.

22.6. It is not to be made to any creature, but to God alone: and, that it may be accepted, it is to be made voluntarily, out of faith, and conscience of duty, in way of thankfulness for mercy received, or for the obtaining of what we want; whereby we more strictly bind ourselves to necessary duties; or to other things, so far and so long as they may fitly conduce thereunto.
Ps. 76:11; Jer. 44:25-26; Deut. 23:21-23; Ps. 50:14; Gen. 28:20-22; 1 Sam. 1:11; Ps. 66:13-14; Ps. 132:2-5.

22.7. No man may vow to do anything forbidden in the Word of God, or what would hinder any duty therein commanded, or which is not in his own power, and for the performance whereof he hath no promise of ability from God. In which respects, Popish monastical vows of perpetual single life, professed poverty, and regular obedience, are so far from being degrees of higher perfection, that they are superstitious and sinful snares, in which no Christian may entangle himself.
Acts 23:12, 14; Mark 6:26; Num. 30:5, 8, 12-13; Matt. 19:11-12; 1 Cor. 7:2, 9; Eph. 4:28; 1 Pet. 4:2; 1 Cor. 7:23.

Chapter 23:
Of the Civil Magistrate

23.1. God, the supreme Lord and King of all the world, hath ordained civil magistrates, to be, under Him, over the people, for His own glory, and the public good; and, to this end, hath armed them with the power of the sword, for the defence and encouragement of them that are good, and for the punishment of evil-doers.
Rom. 13:1-4; 1 Pet. 2:13-14.

23.2. It is lawful for Christians to accept and execute the office of a magistrate, when called thereunto; in the managing whereof, as they ought especially to maintain piety, justice, and peace, according to the wholesome laws of each commonwealth; so for that end, they may lawfully now, under the New Testament, wage war, upon just and necessary occasion.
Prov. 8:15-16; Rom. 13:1-2, 4; Ps. 2:10-12; 1 Tim. 2:2; Ps. 82:3-4; 2 Sam. 23:3; 1 Pet. 2:13; Luke 3:14; Rom. 13:4; Matt. 8:9-10; Acts 10:1-2; Rev. 17:14, 16.

23.3. The civil magistrate may not assume to himself the administration of the Word and sacraments, or the power of the keys of the kingdom of heaven: yet he hath authority, and it is his duty, to take order, that unity and peace be preserved in the Church, that the truth of God be kept pure and entire; that all blasphemies and heresies be suppressed; all corruptions and abuses in worship and discipline prevented or reformed; and all the ordinances of God duly settled, administered and observed. For the better effecting whereof, he hath power to call synods, to be present at them, and to provide, that whatsoever is transacted in them be according to the mind of God.

2 Chron. 26:18 with Matt. 18:17 and Matt. 16:19; 1 Cor. 12:28-29; Eph. 4:11-12; 1 Cor. 4:1-2; Rom. 10:15; Heb. 5:4; Isa. 49:23; Ps. 122:9; Ezra 7:23, 25-28; Lev. 24:16; Deut. 13:5-6, 12; 1 Kings 18:4; 1 Chron. 13:1-9; 2 Kings 23:1-26; 2 Chron. 34:33; 2 Chron. 15:12-13; 2 Chron. 19:8-11; 2 Chron. 29–30; Matt. 2:4-5.

23.4. It is the duty of people to pray for magistrates, to honour their persons, to pay them tribute and other dues, to obey their lawful commands, and to be subject to their authority, for conscience' sake. Infidelity, or difference in religion, doth not make void the magistrates' just and legal authority, nor free the people from their due obedience to them: from which ecclesiastical persons are not exempted; much less hath the Pope any power and jurisdiction over them in their dominions, or over any of their people; and, least of all, to deprive them of their dominions, or lives, if he shall judge them to be heretics, or upon any other pretence whatsoever.
1 Tim. 2:1-2; 1 Pet. 2:17; Rom. 13:6-7; Rom. 13:5; Titus 3:1; 1 Pet. 2:13-14, 16; Rom. 13:1; 1 Kings 2:35; Acts 25:9-11; 2 Pet. 2:1, 10-11; Jude 1:8-11; 2 Thess. 2:4; Rev. 13:15-17.

Westminster Confession of Faith

Chapter 24:
Of Marriage and Divorce

24.1. Marriage is to be between one man and one woman: neither is it lawful for any man to have more than one wife, nor for any woman to have more than one husband; at the same time. Gen. 2:24; Matt. 19:5-6; Prov. 2:17.

24.2. Marriage was ordained for the mutual help of husband and wife, for the increase of mankind with a legitimate issue, and of the Church with an holy seed; and for preventing of uncleanness. *Gen. 2:18; Mal. 2:15; 1 Cor. 7:2, 9.*

Westminster Confession of Faith

24.3. It is lawful for all sorts of people to marry, who are able with judgment to give their consent. Yet is it the duty of Christians to marry only in the Lord: and therefore such as profess the true reformed religion should not marry with infidels, papists, or other idolaters: neither should such as are godly be unequally yoked, by marrying with such as are notoriously wicked in their life, or maintain damnable heresies.
Heb. 13:4; 1 Tim. 4:3; 1 Cor. 7:36-38; Gen. 24:57-58; 1 Cor. 7:39; Gen. 34:14; Ex. 34:16; Deut. 7:3-4; 1 Kings 11:4; Neh. 13:25-27; Mal. 2:11-12; 2 Cor. 6:14.

24.4. Marriage ought not to be within the degrees of consanguinity or affinity forbidden in the Word; nor can such incestuous marriages ever be made lawful by any law of man or consent of parties, so as those persons may live together as man and wife. The man may not marry any of his wife's kindred nearer in blood than he may of his own; nor the woman of her husband's kindred nearer in blood than of her own.
Lev. 18; 1 Cor. 5:1; Amos 2:7; Mark 6:18; Lev. 18:24-28; Lev. 20:19-21.

24.5. Adultery or fornication committed after a contract, being detected before marriage, giveth just occasion to the innocent party to dissolve that contract. In the case of adultery after marriage, it is lawful for the innocent party to sue out a divorce; and, after the divorce, to marry another, as if the offending party were dead.
Matt. 1:18-20; Matt. 5:31-32; Matt. 19:9; Rom. 7:2-3.

24.6. Although the corruption of man be such as is apt to study arguments unduly to put asunder those whom God hath joined together in marriage; yet nothing but adultery, or such wilful desertion as can no way be remedied by the Church or civil magistrate, is cause sufficient of dissolving the bond of marriage; wherein, a public and orderly course of proceeding is to be observed; and the persons concerned in it not left to their own wills and discretion, in their own case.
Matt. 19:8-9; 1 Cor. 7:15; Matt. 19:6; Deut. 24:1-4.

Chapter 25:
Of the Church

25.1. The catholic or universal Church which is invisible, consists of the whole number of the elect, that have been, are, or shall be gathered into one, under Christ the Head thereof; and is the spouse, the body, the fulness of Him that filleth all in all.
Eph. 1:10, 22-23; Eph. 5:23, 27, 32; Col. 1:18.

25.2. The visible Church, which is also catholic or universal under the Gospel (not confined to one nation as before under the law), consists of all those throughout the world that profess the true religion; and of their children: and is the kingdom of the Lord Jesus Christ, the house and family of God, out of which there is no ordinary possibility of salvation.
1 Cor. 1:2; 1 Cor. 12:12-13; Ps. 2:8; Rev. 7:9; Rom. 15:9-12; 1 Cor. 7:14; Acts 2:39; Ezek. 16:20-21; Rom. 11:16; Gen. 3:15; Gen. 17:7; Matt. 13:47; Isa. 9:7; Eph. 2:19; Eph. 3:15; Acts 2:47.

25.3. Unto this catholic visible Church Christ hath given the ministry, oracles, and ordinances of God, for the gathering and perfecting of the saints, in this life, to the end of the world; and doth by His own presence and Spirit, according to His promise, make them effectual thereunto.
1 Cor. 12:28; Eph. 4:11-13; Matt. 28:19-20; Isa. 59:21.

25.4. This catholic Church hath been sometimes more, sometimes less visible. And particular churches, which are members thereof, are more or less pure, according as the doctrine of the Gospel is taught and embraced, ordinances administered, and public worship performed more or less purely in them.
Rom. 11:3-4; Rev. 12:6, 14; Rev. 2–3; 1 Cor. 5:6-7.

25.5. The purest churches under heaven are subject both to mixture and error; and some have so degenerated, as to become no churches of Christ, but synagogues of Satan. Nevertheless, there shall be always a Church on earth, to worship God according to His will.
1 Cor. 13:12; Rev. 2–3; Matt. 13:24-30, 47; Rev. 18:2; Rom. 11:18-22; Matt. 16:18; Ps. 72:17; Ps. 102:28; Matt. 28:19-20.

25.6. There is no other head of the Church, but the Lord Jesus Christ; nor can the Pope of Rome, in any sense, be head thereof; but is that Antichrist, that man of sin, and son of perdition, that exalteth himself, in the Church, against Christ and all that is called God.
Col. 1:18; Eph. 1:22; Matt. 23:8-10; 2 Thess. 2:3-4, 8-9; Rev. 13:6.

Chapter 26:
Of the Communion of Saints

26.1. All saints, that are united to Jesus Christ their Head by His Spirit and by faith, have fellowship with Him in His graces, sufferings, death, resurrection, and glory: and, being united to one another in love, they have communion in each other's gifts and graces, and are obliged to the performance of such duties, public and private, as do conduce to their mutual good, both in the inward and outward man.

1 John 1:3; Eph. 3:16-19; John 1:16; Eph. 2:5-6; Phil. 3:10; Rom. 6:5-6; 2 Tim. 2:12; Eph. 4:15-16; 1 Cor. 12:7; 1 Cor. 3:21-23; Col. 2:19; 1 Thess. 5:11, 14; Rom. 1:11-12, 14; 1 John 3:16-18; Gal. 6:10.

26.2. Saints by profession are bound to maintain a holy fellowship and communion in the worship of God; and in performing such other spiritual services as tend to their mutual edification; as also in relieving each other in outward things, according to their several abilities, and necessities. Which communion, as God offereth opportunity, is to be extended unto all those who, in every place, call upon the name of the Lord Jesus.
Heb. 10:24-25; Acts 2:42, 46; Isa. 2:3; 1 Cor. 11:20; Acts 2:44-45; 1 John 3:17; 2 Cor. 8—9; Acts 11:29-30.

26.3. This communion, which the saints have with Christ, doth not make them, in any wise, partakers of the substance of His Godhead; or to be equal with Christ, in any respect: either of which to affirm is impious and blasphemous. Nor doth their communion one with another, as saints, take away, or infringe the title or property which each man hath in his goods and possessions.
Col. 1:18-19; 1 Cor. 8:6; Isa. 42:8; 1 Tim. 6:15-16; Ps. 45:7 with Heb. 1:8-9; Ex. 20:15; Eph. 4:28; Acts 5:4.

Chapter 27:
Of the Sacraments

27.1. Sacraments are holy signs and seals of the covenant of grace, immediately instituted by God, to represent Christ and His benefits; and to confirm our interest in Him; as also, to put a visible difference between those that belong unto the Church, and the rest of the world; and solemnly to engage them to the service of God in Christ, according to His Word.
Rom. 4:11; Gen. 17:7, 10; Matt. 28:19; 1 Cor. 11:23; 1 Cor. 10:16; 1 Cor. 11:25-26; Gal. 3:17; Rom. 15:8; Ex. 12:48; Gen. 34:14; Rom. 6:3-4; 1 Cor. 10:16, 21.

27.2. There is in every sacrament a spiritual relation, or sacramental union, between the sign and the thing signified; whence it comes to pass, that the names and effects of the one are attributed to the other.
Gen. 17:10; Matt. 26:27-28; Titus 3:5.

27.3. The grace which is exhibited in or by the sacraments rightly used, is not conferred by any power in them: neither doth the efficacy of a sacrament depend upon the piety or intention of him that doth administer it: but upon the work of the Spirit, and the word of institution, which contains, together with a precept authorizing the use thereof, a promise of benefit to worthy receivers.
Rom. 2:28-29; 1 Pet. 3:21; Matt. 3:11; 1 Cor. 12:13; Matt. 26:27-28; Matt. 28:19-20.

27.4. There be only two sacraments ordained by Christ our Lord in the Gospel; that is to say, Baptism and the Supper of the Lord: neither of which may be dispensed by any but by a minister of the Word lawfully ordained.
Matt. 28:19; 1 Cor. 11:20, 23; 1 Cor. 4:1; Heb. 5:4.

27.5. The sacraments of the Old Testament, in regard of the spiritual things thereby signified and exhibited, were, for substance, the same with those of the New.
1 Cor. 10:1-4.

Chapter 28:
Of Baptism

28.1. Baptism is a sacrament of the New Testament, ordained by Jesus Christ, not only for the solemn admission of the party baptized into the visible Church; but also, to be unto him a sign and seal of the covenant of grace, of his ingrafting into Christ, of regeneration, of remission of sins, and of his giving up unto God through Jesus Christ, to walk in newness of life. Which sacrament is, by Christ's own appointment, to be continued in His Church until the end of the world.
Matt. 28:19; 1 Cor. 12:13; Rom. 4:11 with Col. 2:11-12; Gal. 3:27; Rom. 6:5; Titus 3:5; Mark 1:4; Rom. 6:3-4; Matt. 28:19-20.

28.2. The outward element to be used in this sacrament is water, wherewith the party is to be baptized, in the name of the Father, and of the Son, and of the Holy Ghost, by a minister of the Gospel, lawfully called thereunto.
Matt. 3:11; John 1:33; Matt. 28:19-20.

28.3. Dipping of the person into the water is not necessary; but Baptism is rightly administered by pouring or sprinkling water upon the person.
Heb. 9:10, 19-22; Acts 2:41; Acts 16:33; Mark 7:4.

28.4. Not only those that do actually profess faith in and obedience unto Christ, but also the infants of one or both believing parents, are to be baptized.
Mark 16:15-16; Acts 8:37-38; Gen. 17:7, 9-10 with Gal. 3:9, 14, and Col. 2:11-12, and Acts 2:38-39, and Rom. 4:11-12; 1 Cor. 7:14; Matt. 28:19; Mark 10:13-16; Luke 18:15.

28.5. Although it be a great sin to contemn or neglect this ordinance, yet grace and salvation are not so inseparably annexed unto it, as that no person can be regenerated or saved without it; or, that all that are baptized are undoubtedly regenerated.
Luke 7:30 with Ex. 4:24-26; Rom. 4:11; Acts 10:2, 4, 22, 31, 45, 47; Acts 8:13, 23.

Westminster Confession of Faith

28.6. The efficacy of Baptism is not tied to that moment of time wherein it is administered; yet notwithstanding, by the right use of this ordinance, the grace promised is not only offered, but really exhibited and conferred by the Holy Ghost, to such (whether of age or infants) as that grace belongeth unto, according to the counsel of God's own will in His appointed time.
John 3:5, 8; Gal. 3:27; Titus 3:5; Eph. 5:25-26; Acts 2:38, 41.

28.7. The sacrament of Baptism is but once to be administered unto any person.
Titus 3:5.

Chapter 29:
Of the Lord's Supper

29.1. Our Lord Jesus, in the night wherein He was betrayed, instituted the sacrament of His body and blood, called the Lord's Supper, to be observed in His Church, unto the end of the world, for the perpetual remembrance of the sacrifice of Himself in His death; the sealing all benefits thereof unto true believers, their spiritual nourishment and growth in Him, their further engagement in and to all duties which they owe unto Him; and to be a bond and pledge of their communion with Him, and with each other, as members of His mystical body.
1 Cor. 11:23-26; 1 Cor. 10:16-17, 21; 1 Cor. 12:13.

29.2. In this sacrament, Christ is not offered up to His Father; nor any real sacrifice made at all for remission of sins of the quick or dead; but only a commemoration of that one offering up of Himself, by Himself, upon the cross, once for all: and a spiritual oblation of all possible praise unto God for the same: so that the Popish sacrifice of the mass (as they call it) is most abominably injurious to Christ's one, only sacrifice, the alone propitiation for all the sins of His elect.

Heb. 9:22, 25-26, 28; 1 Cor. 11:24-26; Matt. 26:26-27; Heb. 7:23-24, 27; Heb. 10:11-12, 14, 18.

29.3. The Lord Jesus, hath, in this ordinance, appointed His ministers to declare His word of institution to the people; to pray, and bless the elements of bread and wine, and thereby to set them apart from a common to a holy use; and to take and break the bread, to take the cup, and (they communicating also themselves) to give both to the communicants; but to none who are not then present in the congregation.
Matt. 26:26-28, and Mark 14:22-24, and Luke 22:19-20 with 1 Cor. 11:23-26; Acts 20:7; 1 Cor. 11:20.

29.4. Private masses, or receiving this sacrament by a priest or any other alone; as likewise, the denial of the cup to the people, worshipping the elements, the lifting them up or carrying them about for adoration, and the reserving them for any pretended religious use; are all contrary to the nature of this sacrament, and to the institution of Christ.
1 Cor. 10:16; Mark 14:23; 1 Cor. 11:25-29; Matt. 15:9.

29.5. The outward elements in this sacrament, duly set apart to the uses ordained by Christ, have such relation to Him crucified, as that, truly, yet sacramentally only, they are sometimes called by the name of the things they represent, to wit, the body and blood of Christ; albeit in substance and nature they still remain truly and only bread and wine, as they were before.
Matt. 26:26-28; 1 Cor. 11:26-28; Matt. 26:29.

29.6. That doctrine which maintains a change of the substance of bread and wine into the substance of Christ's body and blood (commonly called transubstantiation) by consecration of a priest, or by any other way, is repugnant, not to Scripture alone, but even to common sense and reason; overthroweth the nature of the sacrament, and hath been, and is the cause of manifold superstitions; yea, of gross idolatries.
Acts 3:21 with 1 Cor. 11:24-26; Luke 24:6, 39.

29.7. Worthy receivers outwardly partaking of the visible elements in this sacrament, do then also, inwardly by faith, really and indeed, yet not carnally and corporally, but spiritually, receive and feed upon Christ crucified, and all benefits of His death: the body and blood of Christ being then, not corporally or carnally, in, with, or under the bread and wine; yet, as really, but spiritually, present to the faith of believers in that ordinance, as the elements themselves are to their outward senses.
1 Cor. 11:28; 1 Cor. 10:16.

29.8. Although ignorant and wicked men receive the outward elements in this sacrament: yet they receive not the thing signified thereby, but by their unworthy coming thereunto are guilty of the body and blood of the Lord to their own damnation. Wherefore, all ignorant and ungodly persons, as they are unfit to enjoy communion with Him, so are they unworthy of the Lord's table; and cannot, without great sin against Christ while they remain such, partake of these holy mysteries, or be admitted thereunto.
1 Cor. 11:27-29; 2 Cor. 6:14-16; 1 Cor. 5:6-7, 13; 2 Thess. 3:6, 14-15; Matt. 7:6.

Chapter 30:
Of Church Censures

30.1. The Lord Jesus, as King and Head of His Church, hath therein appointed a government, in the hand of Church officers, distinct from the civil magistrate.
Isa. 9:6-7; 1 Tim. 5:17; 1 Thess. 5:12; Acts 20:17, 28; Heb. 13:7, 17, 24; 1 Cor. 12:28; Matt. 28:18-20.

30.2. To these officers, the keys of the kingdom of heaven are committed: by virtue whereof, they have power respectively to retain, and remit sins; to shut that kingdom against the impenitent, both by the Word and censures; and to open it unto penitent sinners, by the ministry of the Gospel, and by absolution from censures, as occasion shall require.
Matt. 16:19; Matt. 18:17-18; John 20:21-23; 2 Cor. 2:6-8.

30.3. Church censures are necessary, for the reclaiming and gaining of offending brethren, for deterring of others from the like offences, for purging out of that leaven which might infect the whole lump, for vindicating the honour of Christ, and the holy profession of the Gospel, and for preventing the wrath of God, which might justly fall upon the Church, if they should suffer His covenant and the seals thereof to be profaned by notorious and obstinate offenders.
1 Cor. 5; 1 Tim. 5:20; Matt. 7:6; 1 Tim. 1:20; 1 Cor. 11:27-34 with Jude 1:23.

30.4. For the better attaining of these ends, the officers of the Church are to proceed by admonition; suspension from the sacrament of the Lord's Supper for a season; and by excommunication from the Church; according to the nature of the crime, and demerit of the person.
1 Thess. 5:12; 2 Thess. 3:6, 14-15; 1 Cor. 5:4-5, 13; Matt. 18:17; Titus 3:10.

Chapter 31:
Of Synods and Councils

31.1. For the better government, and further edification of the Church, there ought to be such assemblies as are commonly called synods or councils.
Acts 15:2, 4, 6.

Westminster Confession of Faith

31.2. As magistrates may lawfully call a synod of ministers, and other fit persons, to consult and advise with, about matters of religion; so, if magistrates be open enemies to the Church, the ministers of Christ of themselves, by virtue of their office, or they, with other fit persons, upon delegation from their Churches, may meet together in such assemblies.
Isa. 49:23; 1 Tim. 2:1-2; 2 Chron. 19:8-11; 2 Chron. 29–30; Matt. 2:4-5; Prov. 11:14; Acts 15:2, 4, 22-23, 25.

31.3. It belongeth to synods and councils, ministerially to determine controversies of faith and cases of conscience, to set down rules and directions for the better ordering of the public worship of God, and government of His Church; to receive complaints in cases of maladministration, and authoritatively to determine the same: which decrees and determinations, if consonant to the Word of God, are to be received with reverence and submission; not only for their agreement with the Word, but also for the power whereby they are made, as being an ordinance of God appointed thereunto in His Word.
Acts 15:15, 19, 24, 27-31; Acts 16:4; Matt. 18:17-20.

31.4. All synods or councils, since the Apostles' times, whether general or particular, may err; and many have erred. Therefore they are not to be made the rule of faith or practice; but to be used as a help in both.
Eph. 2:20; Acts 17:11; 1 Cor. 2:5; 2 Cor. 1:24.

31.5. Synods and councils are to handle, or conclude, nothing, but that which is ecclesiastical: and are not to intermeddle with civil affairs which concern the commonwealth; unless by way of humble petition, in cases extraordinary; or by way of advice, for satisfaction of conscience, if they be thereunto required by the civil magistrate.
Luke 12:13-14; John 18:36.

Chapter 32:
Of the State of Men After Death, And the Resurrection of the Dead

32.1. The bodies of men, after death, return to dust and see corruption; but their souls (which neither die nor sleep) having an immortal subsistence, immediately return to God who gave them: the souls of the righteous, being then made perfect in holiness, are received into the highest heavens, where they behold the face of God, in light and glory, waiting for the full redemption of their bodies. And the souls of the wicked are cast into hell, where they remain in torments and utter darkness, reserved to the judgment of the great day. Beside these two places, for souls separated from their bodies, the Scripture acknowledgeth none. *Gen. 3:19; Acts 13:36; Luke 23:43; Eccl. 12:7; Heb. 12:23; 2 Cor. 5:1, 6, 8; Phil. 1:23 with Acts 3:21 and Eph. 4:10; Luke 16:23-24; Acts 1:25; Jude 1:6-7; 1 Pet. 3:19.*

32.2. At the last day, such as are found alive shall not die, but be changed: and all the dead shall be raised up, with the selfsame bodies and none other, although with different qualities, which shall be united again to their souls for ever.
1 Thess. 4:17; 1 Cor. 15:51-52; Job 19:26-27; 1 Cor. 15:42-44.

32.3. The bodies of the unjust shall, by the power of Christ, be raised to dishonour; the bodies of the just, by His Spirit, unto honour; and be made conformable to His own glorious body.
Acts 24:15; John 5:28-29; 1 Cor. 15:43; Phil. 3:21.

Chapter 33:
Of the Last Judgment

33.1. God hath appointed a day, wherein He will judge the world in righteousness, by Jesus Christ, to whom all power and judgment is given of the Father. In which day, not only the apostate angels shall be judged, but likewise all persons that have lived upon earth shall appear before the tribunal of Christ, to give an account of their thoughts, words, and deeds; and to receive according to what they have done in the body, whether good or evil.
Acts 17:31; John 5:22, 27; 1 Cor. 6:3; Jude 1:6; 2 Pet. 2:4; 2 Cor. 5:10; Eccl. 12:14; Rom. 2:16; Rom. 14:10, 12; Matt. 12:36-37.

33.2. The end of God's appointing this day is for the manifestation of the glory of His mercy, in the eternal salvation of the elect; and of His justice, in the damnation of the reprobate who are wicked and disobedient. For then shall the righteous go into everlasting life, and receive that fulness of joy and refreshing, which shall come from the presence of the Lord: but the wicked, who know not God, and obey not the Gospel of Jesus Christ, shall be cast into eternal torments, and be punished with everlasting destruction from the presence of the Lord, and from the glory of His power.
Matt. 25:31-46; Rom. 2:5-6; Rom. 9:22-23; Matt. 25:21; Acts 3:19; 2 Thess. 1:7-10.

33.3. As Christ would have us to be certainly persuaded that there shall be a day of judgment, both to deter all men from sin, and for the greater consolation of the godly in their adversity; so will He have that day unknown to men, that they may shake off all carnal security, and be always watchful, because they know not at what hour the Lord will come; and may be ever prepared to say, Come, Lord Jesus, come quickly, Amen.
2 Pet. 3:11, 14; 2 Cor. 5:10-11; 2 Thess. 1:5-7; Luke 21:27-28; Rom. 8:23-25; Matt. 24:36, 42-44; Mark 13:35-37; Luke 12:35-36; Rev. 22:20.

Manufactured by Amazon.ca
Bolton, ON